CW01214950

## FIVE-MINUTE
# BIBLE STORIES

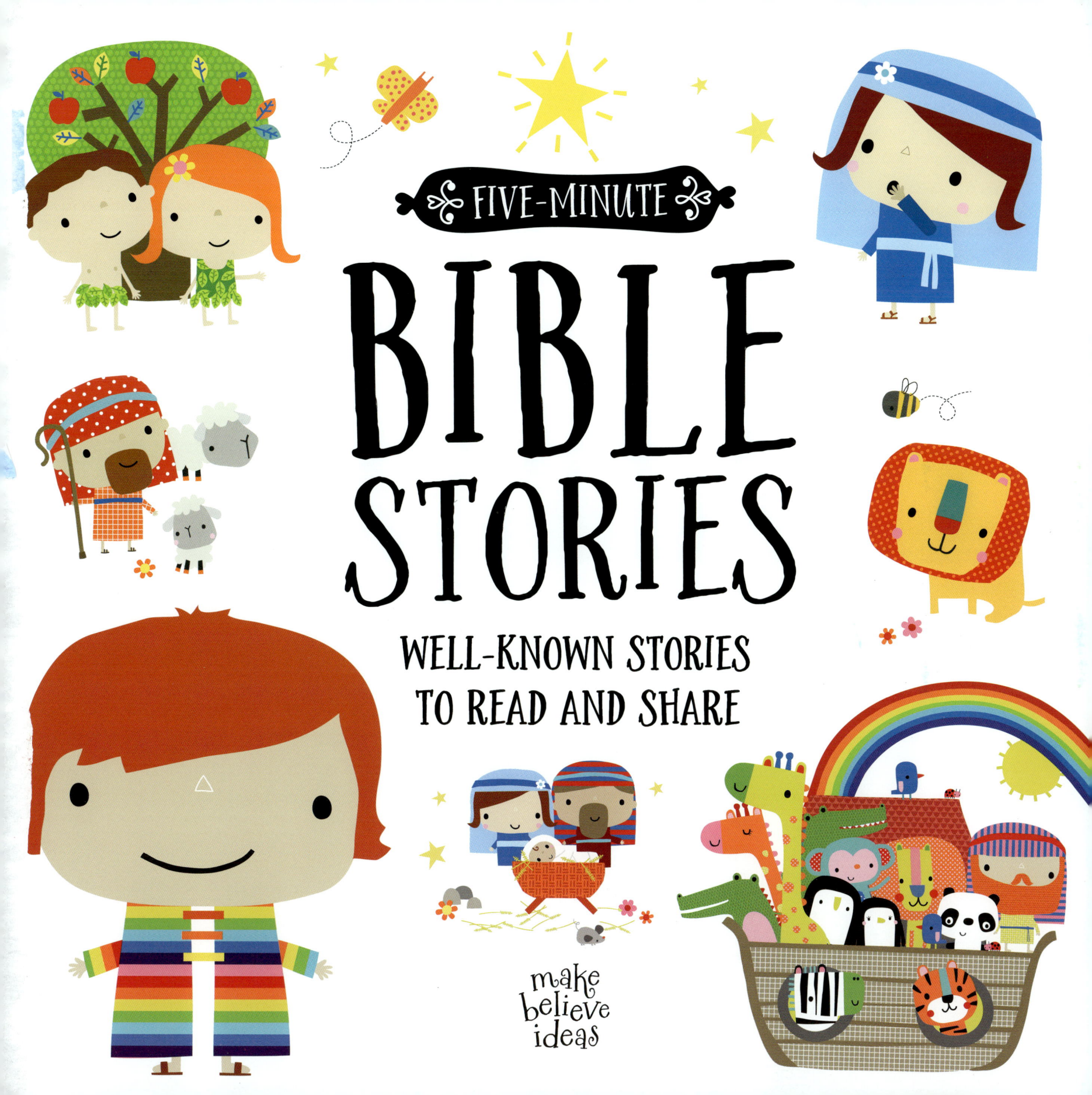

**WELL-KNOWN STORIES TO READ AND SHARE**

make believe ideas

STORIES RETOLD BY FIONA BOON AND HAYLEY DOWN

·

ILLUSTRATED BY DAWN MACHELL

# CONTENTS

**THE OLD TESTAMENT**
**BIBLE STORIES**

CREATION................................................8

NOAH....................................................10

A COLOURFUL COAT......................................12

MOSES...................................................14

DAVID AND GOLIATH....................................16

DANIEL..................................................18

# THE NEW TESTAMENT
## THE STORY OF CHRISTMAS

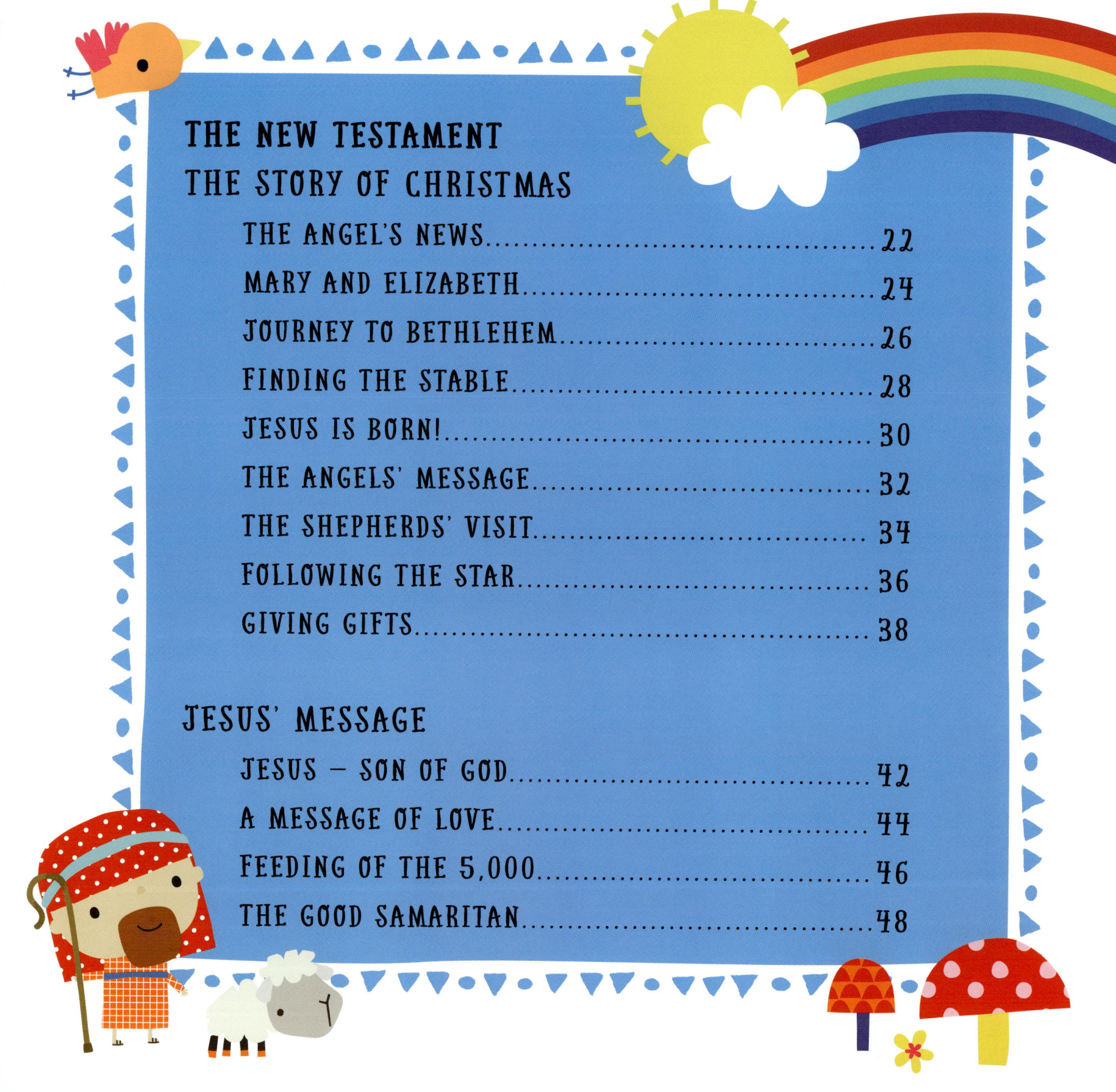

THE ANGEL'S NEWS.................................................22

MARY AND ELIZABETH............................................24

JOURNEY TO BETHLEHEM.........................................26

FINDING THE STABLE..............................................28

JESUS IS BORN!....................................................30

THE ANGELS' MESSAGE...........................................32

THE SHEPHERDS' VISIT............................................34

FOLLOWING THE STAR............................................36

GIVING GIFTS.......................................................38

## JESUS' MESSAGE

JESUS – SON OF GOD.............................................42

A MESSAGE OF LOVE.............................................44

FEEDING OF THE 5,000..........................................46

THE GOOD SAMARITAN..........................................48

## THE STORY OF EASTER

- JESUS AND THE PEOPLE ..................................... 52
- THE LAST SUPPER .......................................... 54
- JESUS PRAYS .............................................. 56
- JESUS IS ARRESTED ........................................ 58
- JESUS IS QUESTIONED ...................................... 60
- THE CRUCIFIXION .......................................... 62
- JESUS IS BURIED .......................................... 64
- JESUS IS ALIVE ........................................... 66
- HOPE FOR US ALL .......................................... 68

## ALL THINGS BRIGHT AND BEAUTIFUL .............. 72

## THE LORD'S PRAYER ............................. 92

# BIBLE
## STORIES

# CREATION

God made **everything** you can see:
the sky, the earth and one **special** tree.
He put **Eve** and **Adam** in a place
where they would **live** in His good grace.

Then a **serpent** tempted **Eve** to **eat** from the forbidden **tree**.

**Adam** and **Eve** left Eden that day, for they had **chosen** their **own** way.

# NOAH

Noah was faithful, true and good.
God told him, "Build an **ark** of wood."
He built the boat and – **two by two** –
brought in **animals** and his **family**, too.

For **forty** days God sent down **rain**,
so the world could **flood** and start again.

Later, when all the land was dry, a rainbow appeared in the sky.

# A COLOURFUL COAT

Old Jacob had **twelve** special sons,

but gave a **coat** to only **one**.

Joseph **dreamt** he would rule one day,

so his brothers sent him **far** away.

But with hard work, he did **succeed** and **helped** people who were in need.

**Pharaoh** dreamt that **famine** would come, but Joseph's plans saved **everyone!**

# MOSES

Moses was found in the water
and taken in by the king's daughter.
But Moses left his wealth and fame
and began to work in God's name.

Pharaoh ignored all God's warnings,
so a new plague came each morning.

God helped Moses to part the sea
and set all of his people free.

# DAVID AND GOLIATH

A war broke out in David's land,
led by Goliath, so tall and grand.
Goliath shouted to the men,
"Beat me, and we won't fight again."

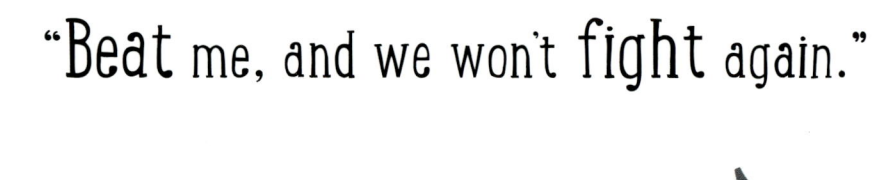

With faith, young David threw a stone,
and Goliath fell down with a groan.
God helped David to win the fight –
proving faith is stronger than might.

# DANIEL

Daniel was **trusted** by the king,
so he looked after **everything**.
But **jealous** men made **prayer** a crime,
then **spied** on Daniel at prayer time.

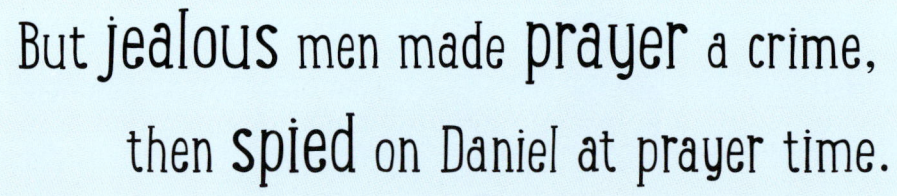

They threw him in the lions' den,
for his prayers had angered them.

But there was no need for alarm;
God kept Daniel safe from harm!

# THE STORY OF CHRISTMAS

# THE ANGEL'S NEWS

An angel flew on golden wings
to tell Mary surprising things:
"My dear, you are God's chosen one –
and you are pregnant with His Son."

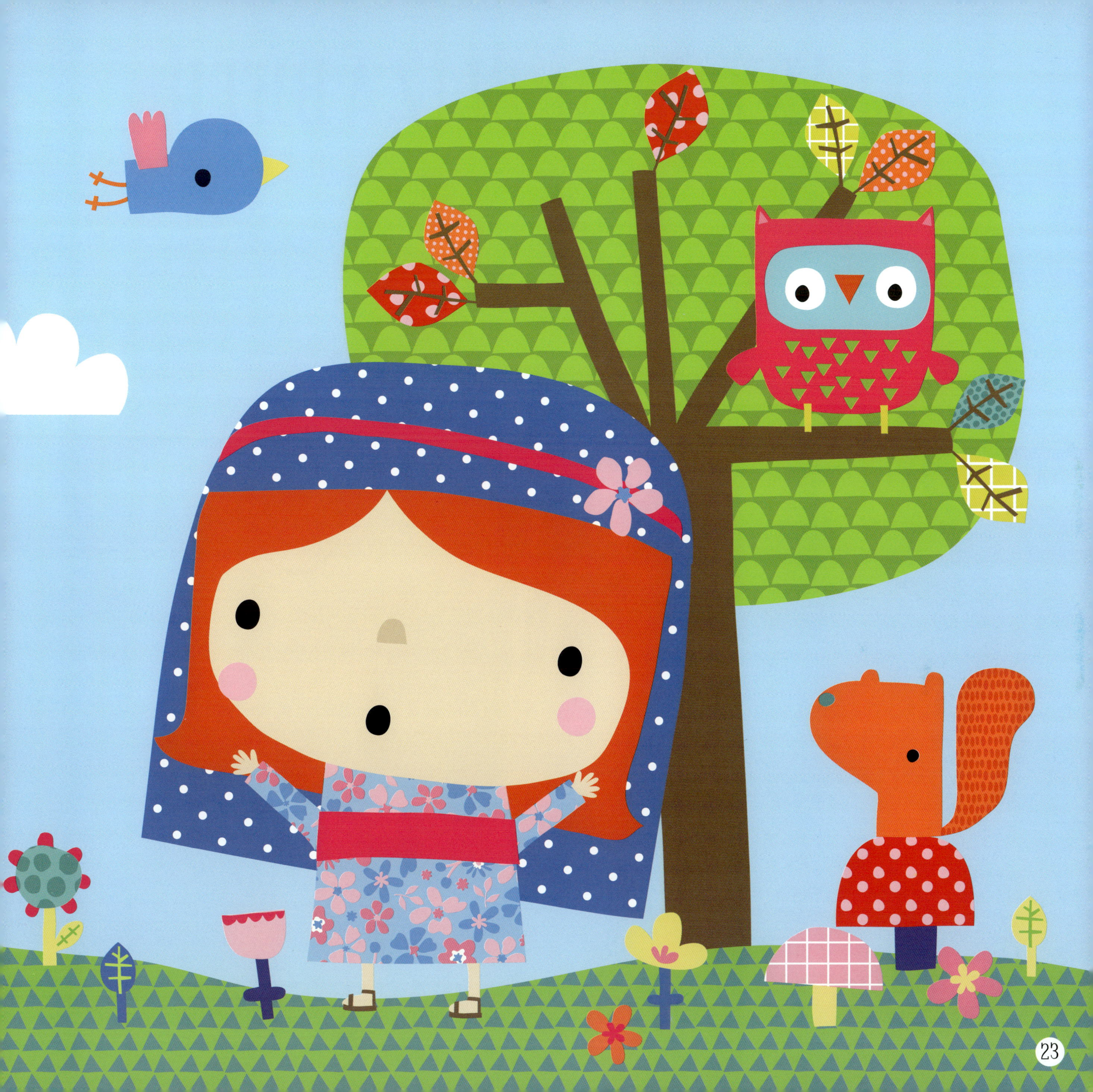

# MARY AND ELIZABETH

Mary's cousin was **pregnant**, too.
When they **met**, Elizabeth knew
Mary was **blessed** by God above,
for her **Son** would **bring** the world such love.

# JOURNEY TO BETHLEHEM

A new **law** meant Joseph must go
on a **trip** that was long and slow.
He took Mary to **Bethlehem**,
with a little **donkey** helping them.

27

# FINDING THE STABLE

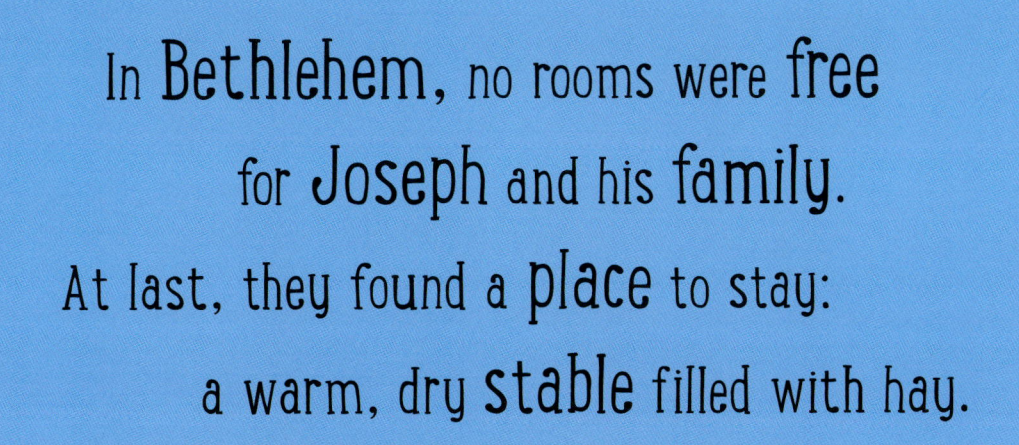

In Bethlehem, no rooms were free
for Joseph and his family.
At last, they found a place to stay:
a warm, dry stable filled with hay.

# JESUS IS BORN!

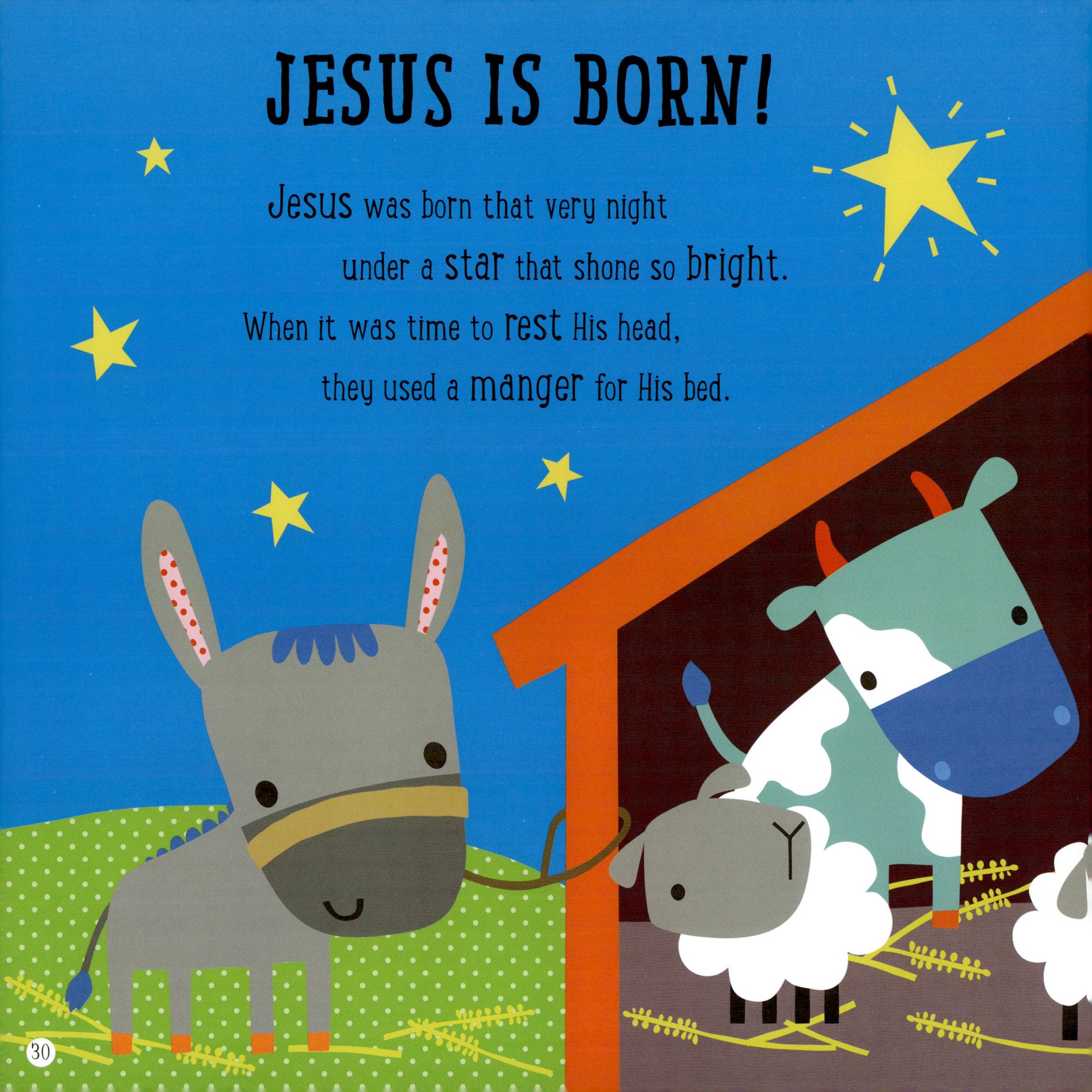

Jesus was born that very night
under a star that shone so bright.
When it was time to **rest** His head,
they used a **manger** for His bed.

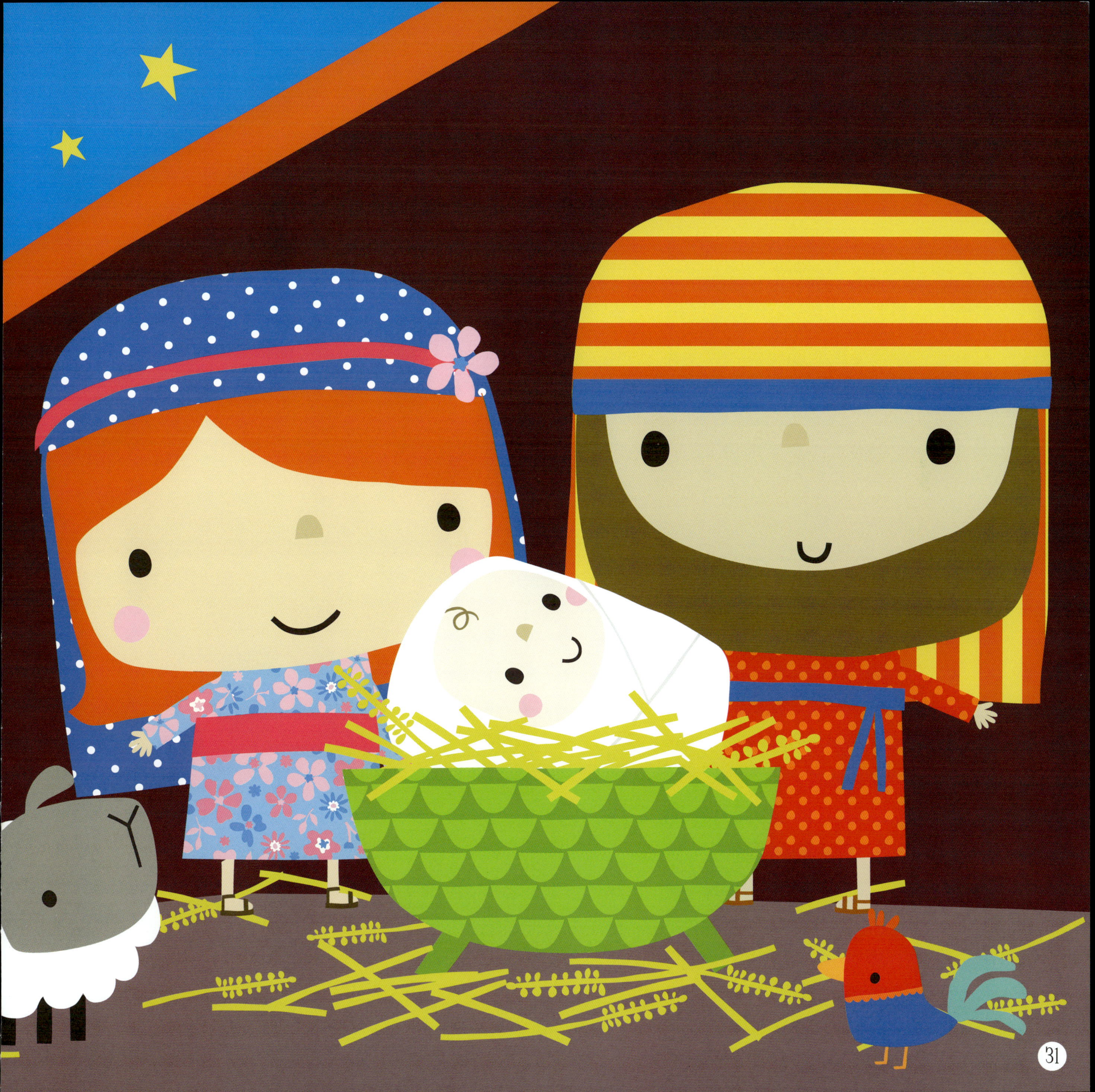

# THE ANGELS' MESSAGE

Outside, some **shepherds** watched their sheep —
careful not to fall **asleep**.
A group of **angels** came to say,
"The Son of God is **born** today!"

# THE SHEPHERDS' VISIT

The shepherds rushed to see the boy,
who was to bring the world such joy.
They left and then told everyone
that they had met God's only Son.

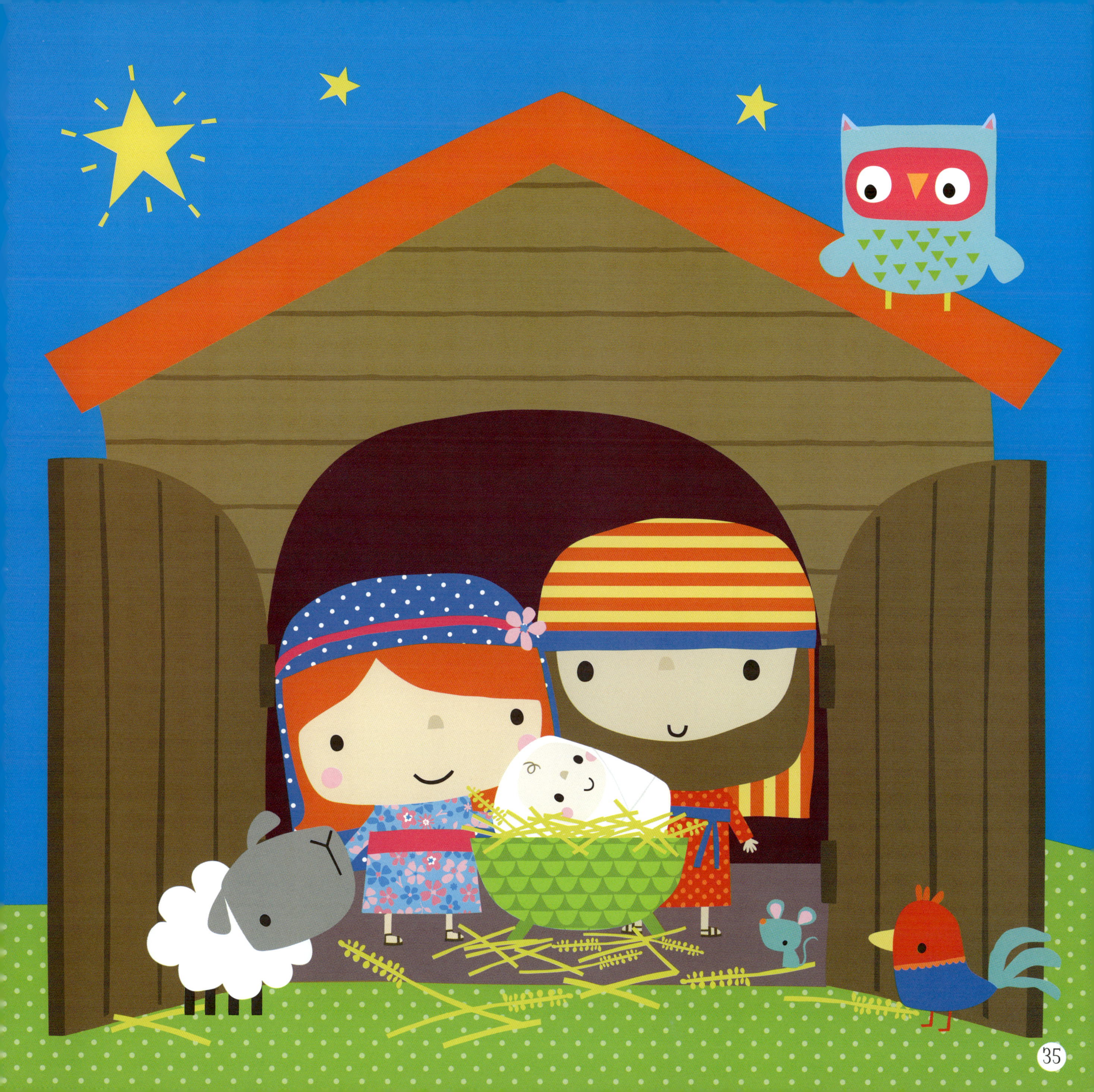

# FOLLOWING THE STAR

Riding camels in lands afar,
wise men saw the shining star.
They went along a dusty road
with special gifts inside their load.

# GIVING GIFTS

They gave him three gifts to behold:

frankincense, myrrh and glinting gold.

The world rejoiced and had no fear,

for now the Son of God was here.

39

# JESUS'
## MESSAGE

# JESUS – SON OF GOD

Jesus grew up and journeyed around
to spread God's Word from town to town.
He came to save us all from sin.
Now we praise and worship Him.

# A MESSAGE OF LOVE

Jesus said to love our sisters and brothers.

In the way He loved us, we should love others.

He taught us the truth and what God's love meant.

Many people followed Him everywhere He went.

45

# FEEDING OF THE 5,000

Five thousand people came one day
to hear what Jesus had to say.
Just as lunchtime had begun,
some had food and some had none.

One small boy had fish and bread –
and with only this, the crowd was fed!
For Jesus performed a miracle,
making food for one and all!

# THE GOOD SAMARITAN

Here's a story that Jesus told:
a man was robbed of clothes and gold.
Two men walked past and heard him yelp,
but neither man stopped by to help.

A Samaritan was passing by
and came to help when he heard the cry!

Kind things like this show us God's love
and the heart of our Father above.

# THE STORY OF
# EASTER

# JESUS AND THE PEOPLE

One day, on a donkey, Jesus entered a great town.

His followers all cheered, but some men wore a frown.

These men hated Jesus and all that He had done.

They were cross when Jesus said He was God's own Son.

# THE LAST SUPPER

Jesus shared a supper with all His closest **friends**.

He knew His time on **earth** was coming to an end.

# JESUS PRAYS

He went into a garden late that night to pray.
Desperate, He said, "Father, is this the only way?"

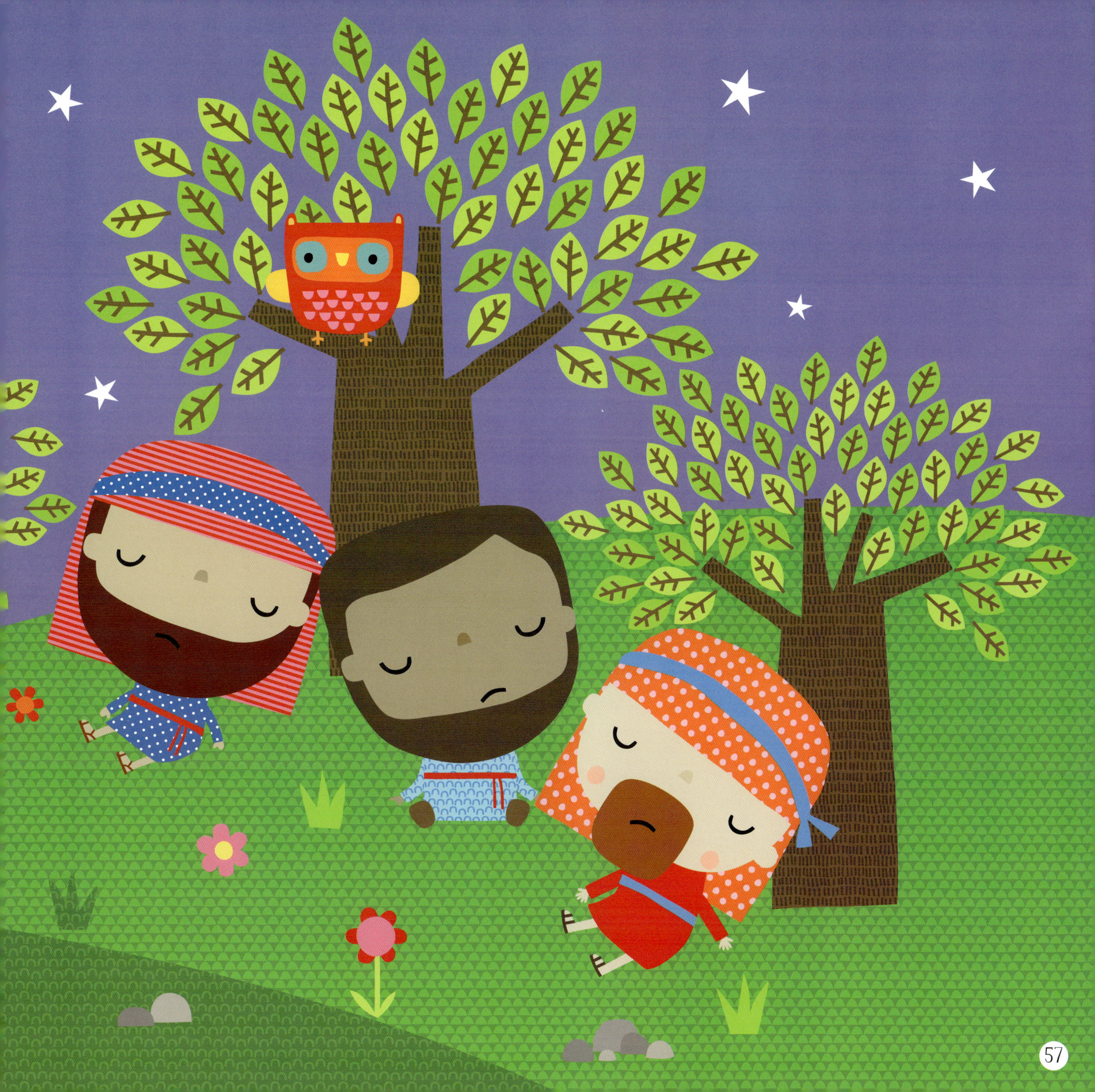

# JESUS IS ARRESTED

The men who hated Jesus found Him **praying** there.

They took Him to be **judged**, even though it was not **fair**.

59

# JESUS IS QUESTIONED

They asked Jesus questions for a very long time
but could not find Him guilty of a single crime.
When the ruler called Pilate wished to set Jesus free,
many in the crowd shouted, "Hang Him on a tree!"

# THE CRUCIFIXION

Jesus was not guilty, but He was put on a cross.

Just as God had told Him: His life must be lost.

63

# JESUS IS BURIED

Suddenly the sky went **dark** and everyone was **scared**.
Six hours later, Jesus **died**, and all His friends despaired.
Some men took His **body** and put it in a cave.
They rolled a stone across to make a sealed **grave**.

# JESUS IS ALIVE

On the third day, to their surprise, the stone had rolled away, and Jesus was alive!

# HOPE FOR US ALL

And all this was God's plan: that Jesus had to die

to pay the price for sin, for all our wrongs and lies.

And so, because of Jesus, when our lives are through,

we can live in heaven if we trust and love Him, too.

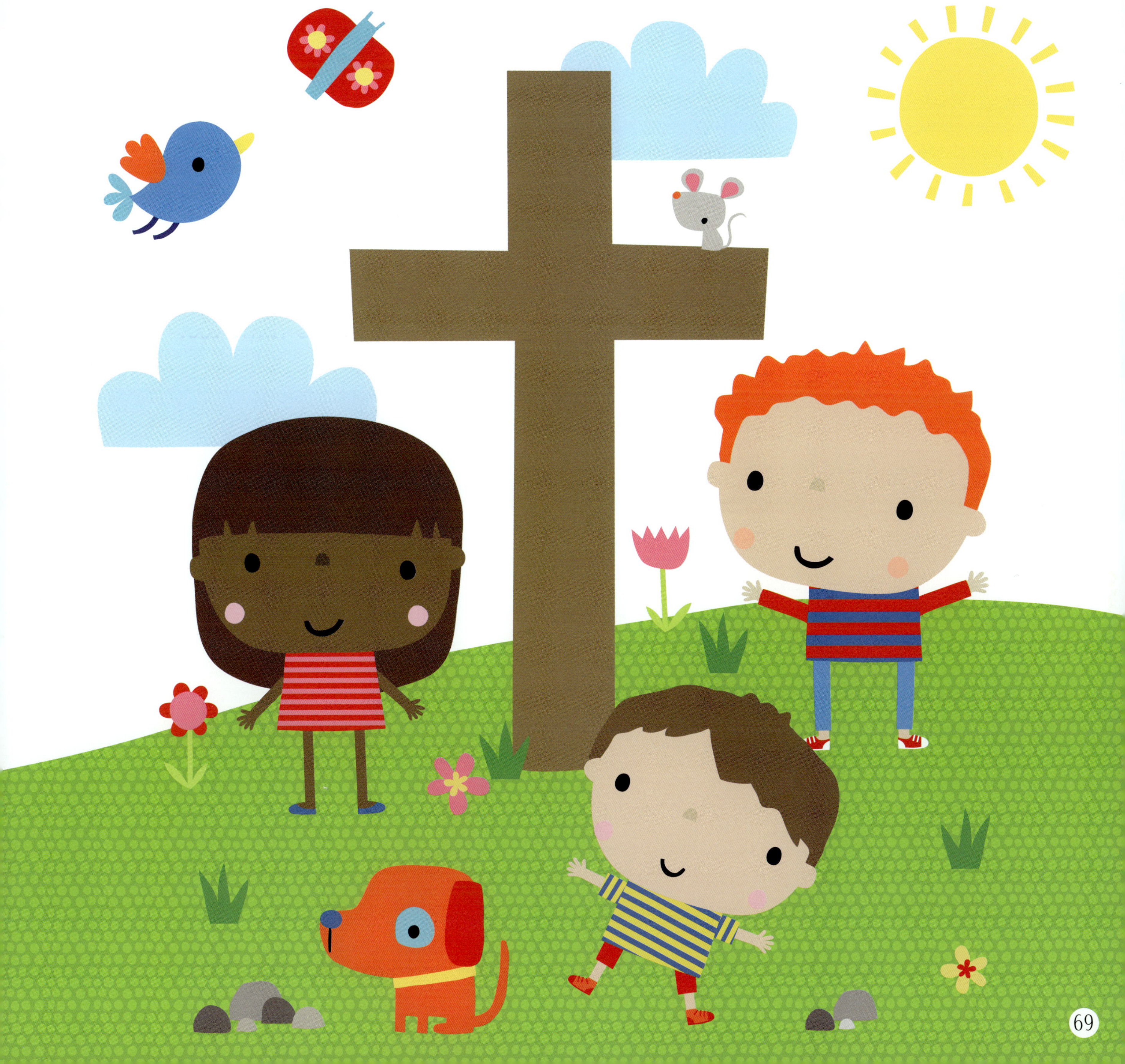

# All Things Bright and Beautiful

All things
BRIGHT
and
BEAUTIFUL,

all creatures
GREAT
and SMALL,

all things WISE and WONDERFUL:

the LORD GOD made them all.

Each little FLOWER that opens,

each little BIRD that sings,

He made their GLOWING COLOURS,

He made their tiny WINGS.

The purple-headed MOUNTAINS,

the RIVER running by,

the SUNSET and the MORNING

that BRIGHTENS up the SKY.

The COLD WIND in the winter,

the pleasant summer SUN,

the ripe
FRUITS
in the GARDEN,

He MADE them, EVERY one.

The TALL TREES in the greenwood,

the MEADOWS where we PLAY,

the RUSHES by the WATER
to GATHER every day.

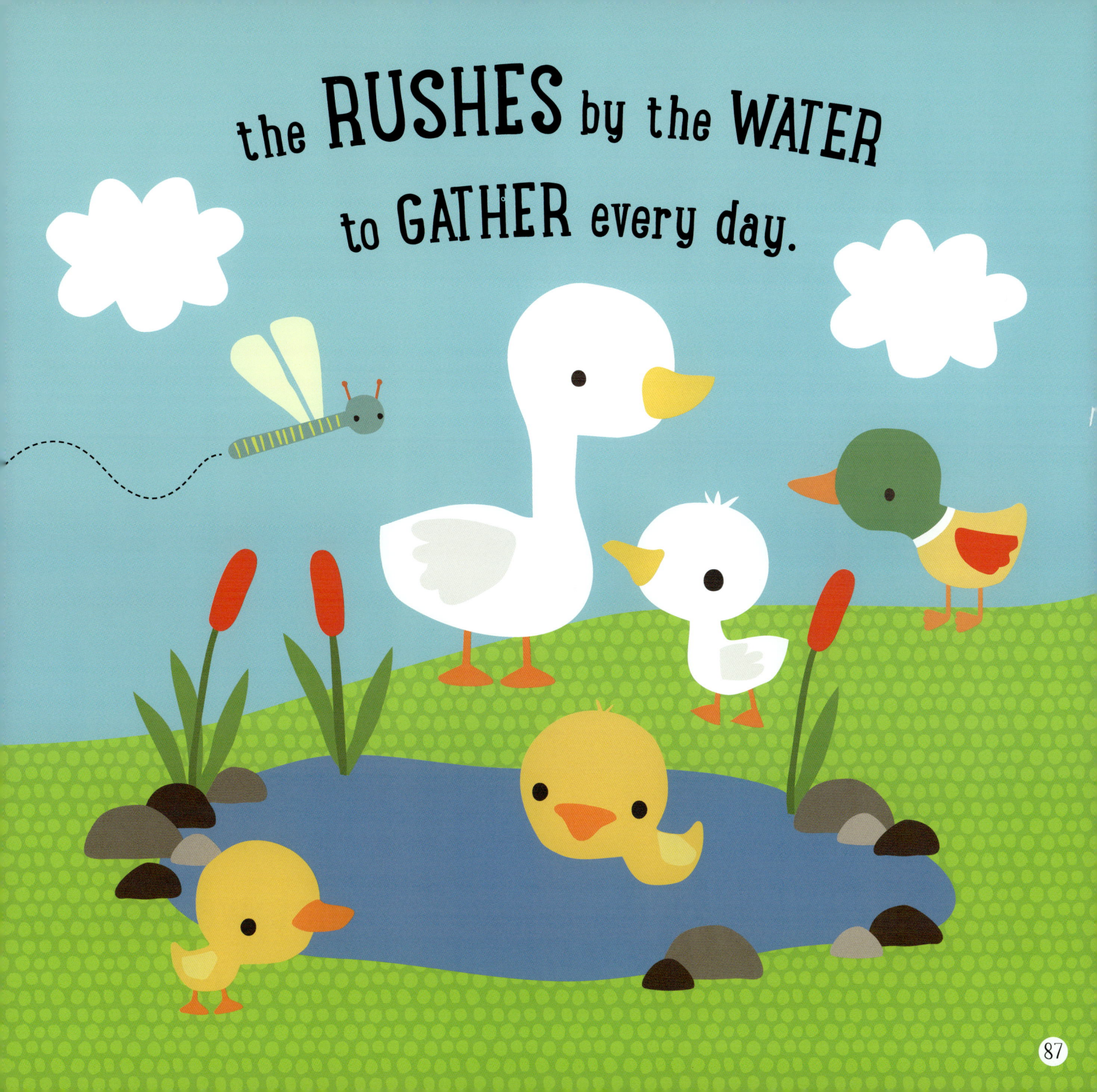

He gave us EYES to SEE THEM,

and LIPS that we might TELL

how GREAT is GOD ALMIGHTY, who has made ALL THINGS well.

All things BRIGHT and BEAUTIFUL, all creatures GREAT and SMALL,

all things WISE and WONDERFUL:

the LORD GOD made them all.

# THE LORD'S PRAYER

Our Father in heaven,
hallowed be Your name.
Your kingdom come,
Your will be done
on earth as in heaven.

Give us today
our daily bread.
Forgive us our sins,
as we forgive those
who sin against us.

Lead us not into **temptation**, but **deliver** us from evil.

For the kingdom, the power and the glory are Yours, now and forever. Amen

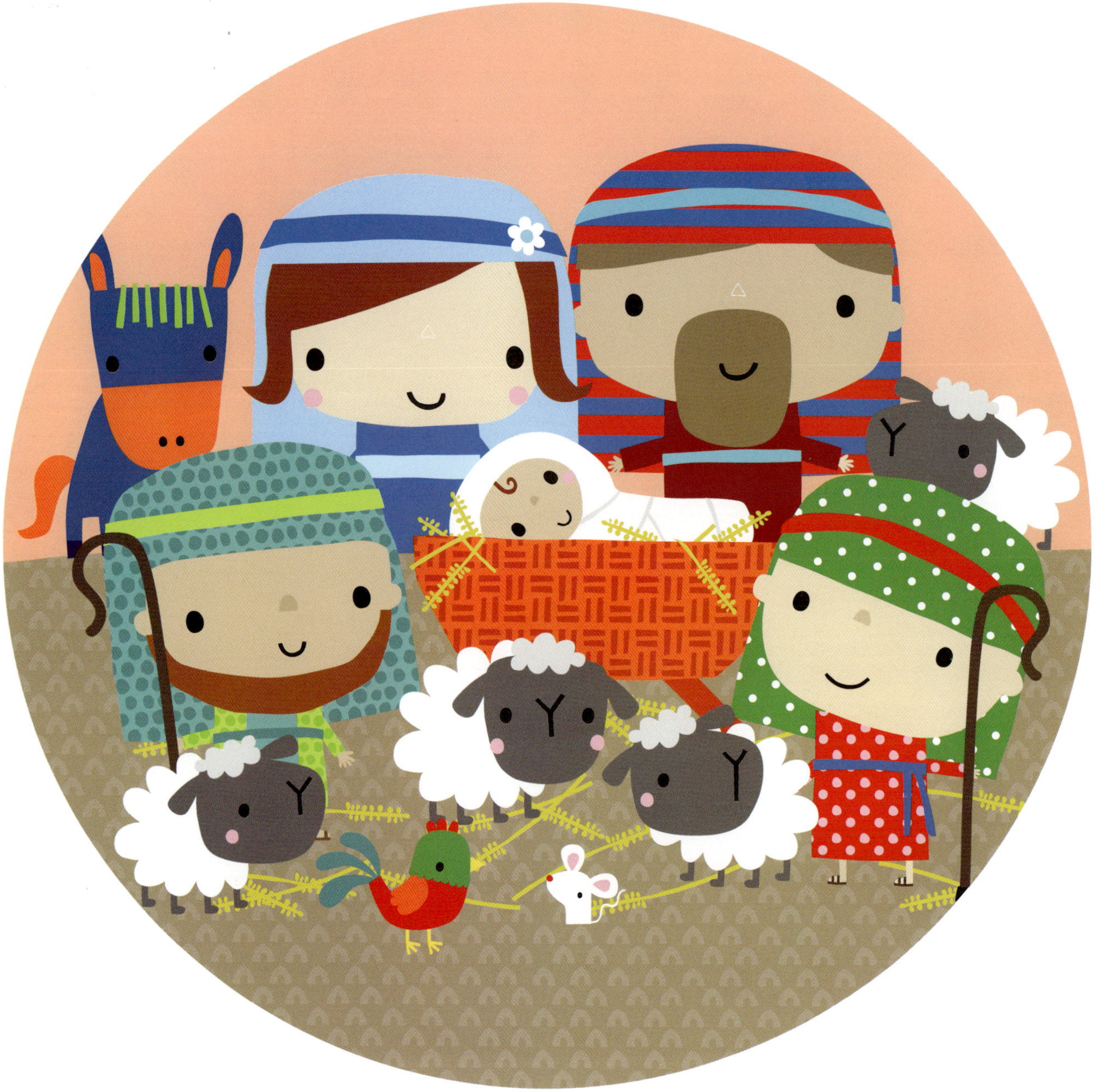